DISCOVER AND DO!

HISTORY

TUDORS

Written by Jane Lacey

Enslow PUBLISHING

Published in 2024 by Enslow Publishing, LLC
2544 Clinton Street
Buffalo, NY 14224

Editor: Izzi Howell
Designer: Clare Nicholas
Series designer: Rocket Design (East Anglia) Ltd

Manufactured in the United States of America

CPSIA compliance information: Batch #CW24ENS: For further information contact
Enslow Publishing LLC, New York, New York at 1-800-398-2504.

Please visit our website, www.enslowpublishing.com. For a free color catalog of all our high-quality books,
call toll free 1-800-398-2504 or fax 1-877-980-4454.666

Cataloging-in-Publication Data

Names: Lacey, Jane.
Title: Tudors / Jane Lacey.
Description: New York : Enslow Publishing, 2024. | Series: Discover and do: history | Includes glossary and index.
Identifiers: ISBN 9781978538320 (pbk.) | ISBN 9781978538337 (library bound) | ISBN 9781978538344 (ebook)
Subjects: LCSH: Great Britain--History--Tudors, 1485-1603--Juvenile literature. | Great Britain--Social life and customs--16th century--Juvenile literature. | Great Britain--Social conditions--16th century--Juvenile literature.
Classification: LCC DA315.L33 2024 | DDC 942.05--dc23

Picture credits:
t=top b=bottom m=middle l=left r=right

Alamy: Colin Waters 22t; Getty: wynnter 9tr, duncan1890 9bl, 18r and 19, NSA Digital Archive 9cr, Macrovector 11, powerofforever 14t, Bettmann 22bl, oscarshost 22br, Elena Istomina 24tr; Shutterstock: walik savitsky cover and 3l, 6b and 29t, Elegant Solution cover and 3r, Annalisa Jones 4, 8t, 8b and 18l, Daria Yakovleva 5tl and 20br, Macrovector 5tr, 14b and 24b, Nadya_Art 5b, 15, 26b, 30b and 31t, Robert Adrian Hillman 6t, Morphart Creation 9tl, 9br and 20bl, Vectorpocket 10t, Mistervlad 10b, Pav-Pro Photography Ltd 12t and 32, Brooks Original Photos 12b, benchart 13t, Photographee.eu 13b, Vasilinka 16tl, Richard Hayman 16tr and 30t, Lemberg Vector studio 16b and 31b, Annas_ Kurniawan, Sketch Master and Ysami 20t, delcarmat 20cr, Axel Redder 21, Tartila 24tl, 29b and 31c, Green Cactus 25, delcarmat 26t and 28, Claudio Divizia 27.

All design elements from Shutterstock.
Craft models from a previous series made by Anna-Marie D'Cruz/photos by Steve Shott.

DISCOVER AND DO!

HISTORY

TUDORS

Written by Jane Lacey

Enslow PUBLISHING

CONTENTS

Words that appear in **bold** can be found in the glossary on pages 28–29.

THE TUDORS

Five Tudor kings and queens ruled England for 118 years from 1485 to 1603.

Wars of the Roses

Between 1455 and 1485, two families, called the House of York and the House of Lancaster, fought for the throne of England. Their family **emblems** were roses; a red rose for Lancaster and a white rose for York. The fight for the throne became known as the Wars of the Roses.

Tudor Rose

In 1485, Henry Tudor, of the House of Lancaster, defeated King Richard III and became King Henry VII. He married Elizabeth of York and combined the two roses to make a new emblem—the Tudor rose.

ACTIVITY

MAKE A STAINED-GLASS ROSE WINDOW

Ask an adult to help you with this activity.

You will need:

- **colored paper (black, gold, white, red, and green)**
- **dinner plate (to trace)**
- **scissors**
- **pencil**
- **tissue paper, various bright colors**
- **glue**

1 Draw around a dinner plate on thin black paper and cut out. the circle Fold the circle in half, then in half again, and then repeat.

2 Copy these shapes onto the folded paper. Ask an adult to help you cut them out. Open up the circle.

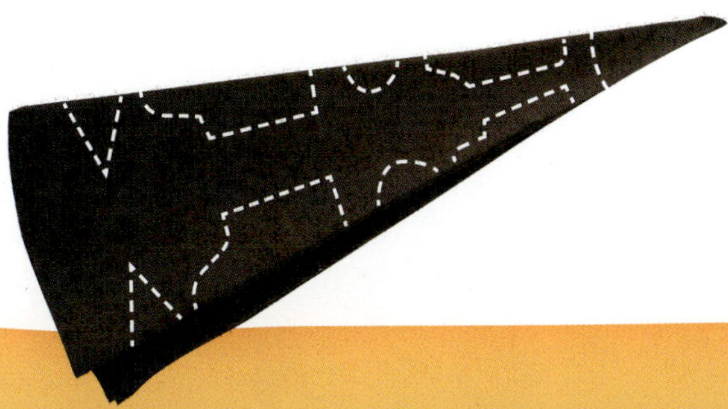

3 Stick brightly colored tissue paper over the holes on one side with glue.

4 Make a Tudor rose to go in the center with gold, white, and red paper. Add four green leaves around the rose before gluing it in the middle.

HENRY VIII

Henry VIII became king when he was only 17 after the death of his father, Henry VII.

Henry VIII loved hunting, sports, and rich banquets. He wanted to be seen as a powerful king in Europe as well as at home. He longed for a son and **heir** to the throne. Henry VIII is famous for having been married six times.

The six wives of Henry VIII

Catherine of Aragon

Henry's first wife was Catherine of Aragon. She had six children, but five died young. Only one daughter, Mary, survived. Henry **divorced** Catherine so he could marry Anne Boleyn.

Anne Boleyn

Anne Boleyn had a daughter, Elizabeth, but no son. Henry believed she had been **unfaithful** and she was **executed**.

Jane Seymour

Jane Seymour died after giving birth to a son, Edward, who became King Edward VI.

Anne of Cleves

Anne of Cleves was a German princess. Henry divorced her after only six months of marriage.

Catherine Howard

Catherine Howard was 30 years younger than Henry when they married. She was unfaithful to Henry, and he ordered her to be executed.

Catherine Parr

Catherine Parr looked after Henry and his three children until he died in 1543.

LIFE AT COURT

Henry VIII's **court** was wherever he was living at the time. It could be at any of his many palaces. He traveled between palaces with his **courtiers** and servants and stayed for about three months before moving on.

Henry served his guests huge feasts with many expensive dishes.

International visitors

To show how powerful he was, Henry entertained important people from many countries. He impressed his visitors with sports, music, dance, and poetry.

Hampton Court Palace

Hampton Court was one of Henry's six London palaces. It had three big kitchens where meals for as many as 1,000 people were cooked. Rich tapestries and grand portraits hung on the walls.

Hampton Court was one of Henry VIII's favorite palaces.

Palace gardens

Guests could stroll in the beautiful gardens of his palaces among fountains and flowerbeds. They might even get lost in a maze. Hedge mazes were popular in Tudor gardens. You had to find your way along the paths to the center—then out again!

Some mazes had a surprise in the center, such as a special plant or a fountain.

ACTIVITY

DESIGN A MAZE

You will need:

- **green modeling clay**
- **cardboard**
- **green paint**

1. Roll out long sausages of green modeling clay. Flatten them so they stand up like hedges.

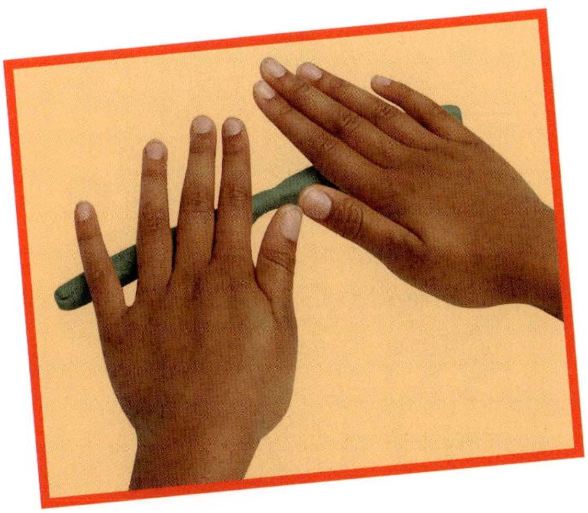

2. Paint a piece of cardboard green. Lay out the modeling clay to form a maze. Smooth out the places where the "hedges" meet.

3. See if your friends can find their way to the center of your maze.

TUDOR HOMES

Only the royal family and nobles lived in palaces and grand houses.

Middle-class Tudors, such as farmers, doctors, and **lawyers**, lived comfortably. But life could be hard for servants and laborers who were often very poor.

This is what the bedroom in the house of a very rich Tudor would have looked like.

Furniture

An ordinary Tudor home would have just a few pieces of furniture, usually made of wood, and useful things such as bedding, pots, and tools.

This is what the main room in an ordinary Tudor house would have looked like.

Inventories

An inventory is a list of someone's belongings. People made inventories to record what they owned. Inventories tell us interesting things about them. When he died, Edward Jaxson owned one broken table, two old carpenter's chairs, three mattresses, and 30 acres (12 ha) of corn. So we know that he owned land in the country but he wasn't rich.

Items such as chairs were included in inventories.

ACTIVITY

MAKE AN INVENTORY

Margery Wren owned 10 featherbeds, 20 pairs of linen sheets, 48 bowls, many cows, sheep, and pigs, 2 plows, and a money chest.

1. What do her belongings tell you about her?

2. Make an inventory of the things in your bedroom.

If someone found it in 500 years' time, what would they learn about you?

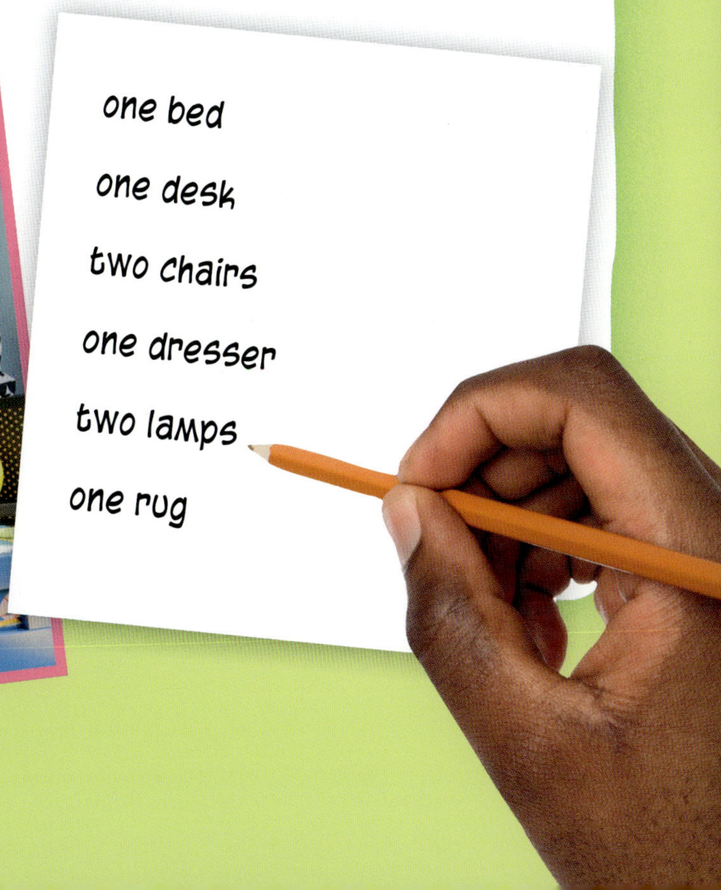

TUDOR LONDON

Tudor London was a busy city and port. Ships sailed up and down the River Thames bringing **goods** from abroad. Rich **merchants** lived in large houses but many of the streets were crowded and smelly. Trash was thrown out onto the streets and into the river as there was nowhere to put it.

The streets of Tudor London were dirty and busy with lots of people.

Plague

Rats with fleas scurried from house to house. Drinking water was dirty. Many people died of the **plague** in Tudor London as disease spread quickly. People carried flaming torches and sweet-smelling pomanders of herbs and spices through the stinking London streets to protect themselves from the awful smell and disease.

The Tower of London was a prison as well as a palace. Traitors who plotted against the king or queen were executed there.

The Tower of London still stands in London, United Kingdom.

ACTIVITY

MAKE A POMANDER

You will need:

- **light cloth (at least 8 by 8 inches [20 x 20 cm])**
- **scissors**
- **dried flower petals**
- **slivers of dried lemon and orange peel**
- **selection of dried herbs and spices**
- **ribbon**

1. Cut a square of light cloth such as muslin, 8 x 8 inches (20 x 20 cm).

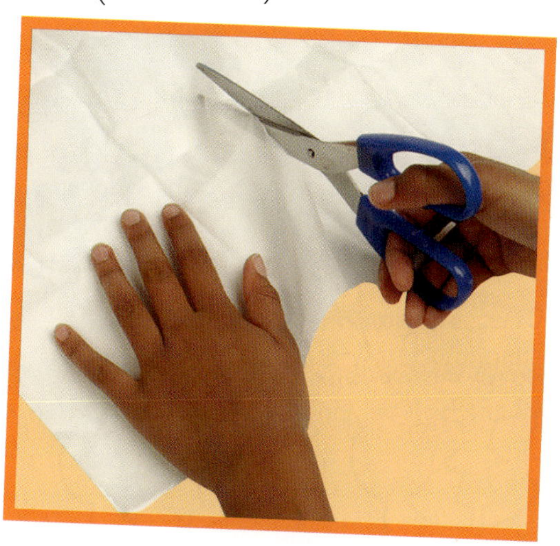

2. Collect dried petals of scented flowers such as roses, jasmine, and lavender. You will also need slivers of lemon and orange peel and some herbs and spices.

3. Put a handful of dried petals on the square of cloth. Add two bay leaves, a pinch of rosemary, a few cloves, and the slices of peel.

4. Gather the corners of the cloth together and twist in the middle. Secure with a length of ribbon.

STREET LIFE

There were no police on the Tudor streets to protect people. Rich people had to guard their money as pickpockets lay in wait. It was against the law to beg but people often did.

These almshouses in Stratford-upon-Avon were used in the 16th century.

Homes for the poor

Rich people were expected to give alms to the deserving poor, such as the old or sick. **Almshouses** were built to give poor people somewhere to live.

Street entertainment

Jesters, jugglers, and **minstrels** could earn money by entertaining the crowds at festivals and even public executions.

The cries of street sellers advertised hot pies, baked meats and apples, bread, fruit, and fresh fish for sale.

ACTIVITY

MAKE A JESTER'S HAT

You will need:

- **paper, various bright colors**
- **tape**
- **glue**
- **bells or pom-poms to decorate**

1. On paper, make four copies of the shape below (about the size of this page); use two different colors. Make two copies in each color.

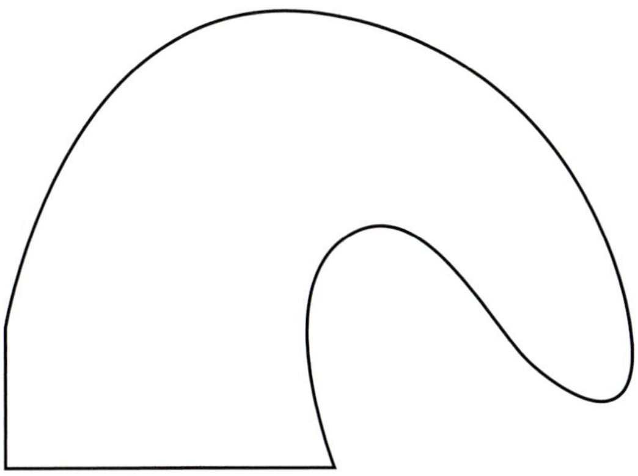

2. Tape the sides together, as shown below. Then tape the ends so that it fits around your head.

3. Glue the points of the hat together at the very ends.

4. Add bells, pom-poms, or whatever you have to the points of the hat. Now it's ready to wear!

ELIZABETH I

Elizabeth I's reign lasted for 45 years and is sometimes called a "golden age." During this time, England became strong and powerful.

Elizabeth was popular with her people and never married. She said she was married to the "kingdom of England."

Plots

Many **plots** were made to overthrow Elizabeth. She had to be strong and **ruthless** to hold onto power. Her cousin, Mary Queen of Scots, plotted against her and Elizabeth had her executed.

Mary Queen of Scots

The Great Seal

The Great Seal was stamped onto letters and documents to prove they had the royal "seal of approval." Elizabeth's seal showed her crowned and holding an **orb and scepter**.

This is a drawing of Elizabeth's seal.

ACTIVITY

DESIGN AND MAKE A SEAL

Design your own seal. Think about what you want to show on it and why.

You will need:

- **pencil**
- **paper (about 2.5 inches [6 cm] in diameter)**
- **air-drying clay**
- **water**
- **modeling tools**
- **modeling clay**

1. Plan your design in pencil in a circle on paper—about 2.5 inches (6 cm) in diameter. Make a cylinder of air-hardening clay in the same size.

2. Using another piece of clay, cut out the shapes for your design. Moisten the clay with water and stick the shapes onto the cylinder.

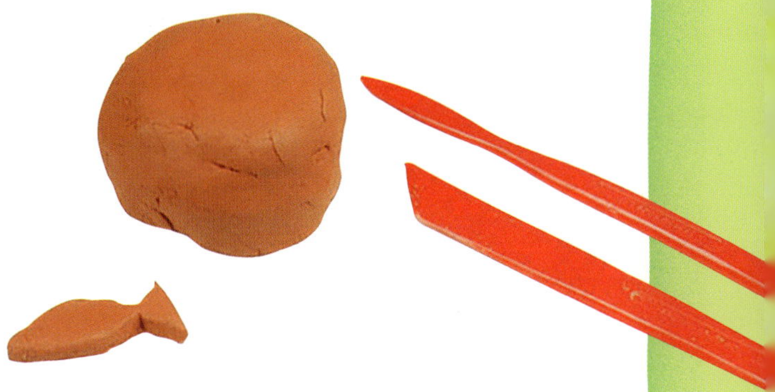

3. Leave the clay to dry. Then, stamp your seal into a blob of modeling clay to leave the impression on it.

EXPLORATION

During Tudor times, explorers sailed the oceans to discover new lands. They returned from Asia and North America with silks, spices, tobacco, pineapples, tomatoes, and potatoes—fruits and vegetables that had never been seen in England before.

Danger at sea

Sailors were often in danger from storms, hunger and thirst, disease, and pirates. Sir Francis Drake became rich by attacking Spanish ships and robbing them of gold and goods. He was also the first Englishman to sail around the world. It took him four years.

Pirates attacked ships carrying valuable treasure from North and South America to Europe.

Sir Walter Raleigh

Sir Walter Raleigh sailed to North America. He claimed land there for England.

Sir Walter Raleigh also explored some parts of South America.

Sailors looked out for the North Star to help them navigate their way round the world. It is always in the north.

The North Star is quite bright and is easy to spot in the constellation Ursa Minor.

ACTIVITY

MAKE A STAR MAP

You will need:

- **black card stock**
- **dinner plate (to trace)**
- **pencil**
- **silver pen**
- **silver star stickers (optional)**

1. Draw around a dinner plate on some black card stock and cut out. Copy the stars shown below onto the card stock in pencil.

2. Join the stars in each constellation with a silver pen line.

3. Stick silver stars on the brightest stars. Make a silver blob on less bright stars.

4. On a bright night, look at the stars and see if you can find the stars on your map. You can also look at websites to see more stars: *stardate.org/nightsky/constellations*.

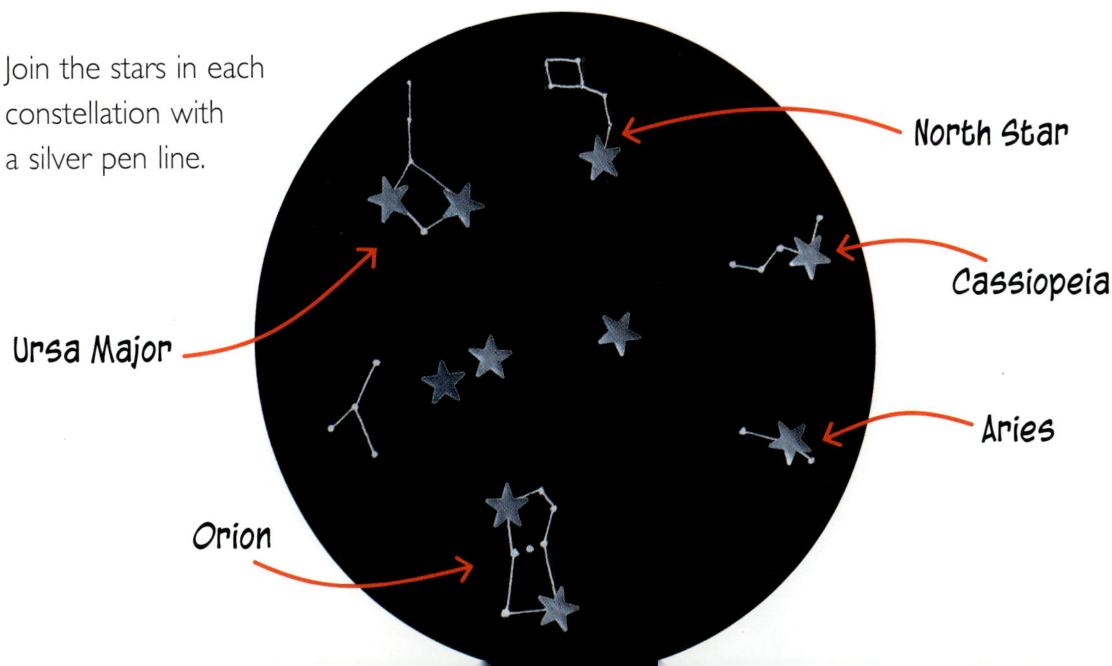

TUDOR CHILDHOOD

Boys from wealthy homes went to school or were taught at home. Girls learned to be wives and housekeepers. Village boys could go to their local petty school and learn to read and write. Some went on to grammar schools.

This engraving shows a Tudor classroom.

Jobs for children

Poor children often had to work to bring in money for their families. Between the ages of 7 and 9, boys began to learn a trade and girls became servants. Children in the countryside worked in the fields. Girls could marry when they were only 12 years old.

Children learned to read from a hornbook made from very thin horn-covered paper.

Toys and games

Only rich children had well-made toys. Poorer children played together in the fields and streets. They made hoops, skittles and balls, and marbles from old barrels, rags, sticks, clay, or whatever they could find.

Tudor children made marbles from clay.

ACTIVITY

MAKE AND PLAY SKITTLES

You will need:

- **five small screw-top plastic bottles**
- **paints or paper, various colors**
- **water**
- **strips of rag**

1. Collect five small plastic bottles with screw-top lids. Decorate them with paint or colored paper.

2. Put a little water in the bottles and screw on the lids. Make a ball with strips of rags, about 8 inches x 1 inch (20 cm x 3 cm) strips.

3. Use one strip to tie them tightly round the middle. Spread out the strips to make a ball.

4. Arrange the skittles in a triangle. Take turns with your friends to knock them down with the rag ball.

FOOD

Tudor kings and queens impressed their foreign guests with expensive banquets. Wild boar, deer, beef, lamb, fish, and all kinds of birds including swans and peacocks were served. Marzipan made from sugar, almonds, and rose water was molded into animal and flower shapes.

Many different types of food and drink were served at Tudor banquets.

Everyday food

Ordinary people ate turnips, cabbage, and beans. They ate bread at every meal. In the country, they might catch rabbits, wild birds, and fish to eat. In the towns, street traders sold hot pies, sausages, and baked apples.

The Tudors mostly drank beer with their meals. Water from lakes and rivers was too dirty to drink and would have made them ill.

Keeping food fresh

In the past, it was difficult to keep food fresh. Meat was salted to stop it from going bad. Fruit was made into jam, and vegetables were pickled.

Curds

In Tudor times, curds were made from heating buttermilk, (the liquid left over after making butter), and milk straight from the cow. When it thickened, it was strained, then cooled. Lemon and honey and thick cream were added to make lemon curd.

ACTIVITY

MAKE A MODERN LEMON CURD

Ask an adult to help you with this activity.

You will need:

- **3/4 cup white sugar**
- **3/4 cup fresh lemon juice**
- **three large eggs**
- **1/2 cup unsalted butter**
- **1 tablespoon grated lemon zest**

1. Finely grate the lemon rind and put it into a heavy-bottomed saucepan. Add the sugar and mix together.
2. Squeeze the lemon juice into a bowl and add the eggs. Whisk them together and pour the mixture over the sugar. Mix them over medium heat.
3. Cut the butter into small pieces and add them to the mixture. Stir for about 10 minutes until the lemon curd is thick and smooth.
4. You can have your lemon curd on toast or bake it in some pastry shells to make lemon curd tarts.

THEATER

All over England, plays were performed by actors in barns and courtyard inns, and in the halls of great houses and universities. In Tudor London, there were theaters such as the Swan, the Rose, and the Globe. Audiences paid a penny to stand in the open air to see a play or paid more for a seat in the gallery.

Acting

Actors wore Tudor clothes, whatever the play. Women were not allowed to perform so males played women's roles. Scenery and **props** were very simple.

William Shakespeare

William Shakespeare wrote popular plays that are still performed in theaters today.

Shakespeare wrote nearly 40 plays and over 150 poems.

The original Globe theater opened in 1598. Many of Shakespeare's plays were performed there.

In 1997, the Globe theater was rebuilt as it would have been in Tudor times.

ACTIVITY

MAKE A MODEL OF THE GLOBE THEATER

You will need:

- **cream-colored card stock**
- **scissors**
- **pens or paint, various colors**
- **glue and/or tape**
- **art straws**
- **small carboard box**

1. Fold down 1.5 inches (3.5 cm) at the top and bottom of the cream-colored card stock. Snip from the edge to the folds 4 inches (10 cm) in from the side in four places as shown. Fold side panels in.

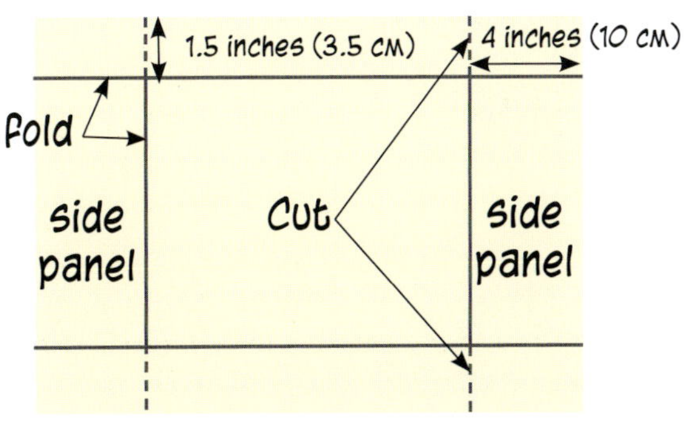

2. Draw or paint on the galleries and audience on the side panels. Bend the card stock around and glue or tape the card stock where you cut it in place. Stick cut art straws along the top fold to make the thatched roof.

3. Paint a small box for the stage. Fold a rectangle of card stock 6 x 2.5 inches (15 x 6 cm) and stick on cut art straws for the stage canopy. Attach the canopy to the stage using art straws as pillars.

Glossary

almshouse

An almshouse was a house built to give poor people somewhere to live.

court

A court is the place where a king or queen lived together with their officials.

courtier

A courtier is someone who attended the king or queen's court.

divorce

To divorce is to end a marriage legally.

emblem

An emblem is a symbol or a badge.

execute

To execute someone is to kill him or her as a punishment.

goods

Goods are things that are bought and sold.

grammar school

A grammar school is a type of secondary school.

heir

An heir is the person who will become king or queen when the existing king or queen dies.

jester

A jester is someone who entertained people, often at the royal court.

lawyer

A lawyer is someone who is an expert in the law and helps people with legal matters.

merchant

A merchant is a person who buys and sells things.

minstrel

A minstrel was a musician who traveled around the country.

noble

A noble is someone from the upper classes, who often owned a lot of land.

orb and scepter

An orb is a globe with a cross on top. A scepter is a long, decorated staff. These were both used by a king or qiueen as symbols of power.

petty school

A petty school was a school at the house of a well-educated woman. Children were taught to read and write, and how to behave.

pickpocket

A pickpocket is someone who is good at stealing things from people's pockets.

plague

The plague is a dangerous illness that spread by flea bites. The plague killed many people in Tudor times.

plot

A plot is a secret plan.

props

Props are objects used in a play.

reign

A reign is the time when someone is king or queen.

ruthless

Ruthless describes someone who is cruel and who has no pity.

unfaithful

Unfaithful describes someone who has a romantic relationship with someone other than who they are married to.

Quiz

1. **Which two families fought in the Wars of the Roses?**
   a) the House of Tudor and the House of London
   b) the House of Windsor and the House of Bristol
   c) the House of Scotland and the House of England
   d) the House of York and the House of Lancaster

2. **How many Tudor kings and queens were there?**
   a) three
   b) five
   c) six
   d) eight

3. **Who was the first wife of Henry VIII?**
   a) Anne Boleyn
   b) Catherine Parr
   c) Catherine of Aragon
   d) Anne of Cleves

4. **Where were traitors executed in London?**
   a) the River Thames
   b) the Tower of London
   c) Hampton Court
   d) Westminster Abbey

5. **What was an almshouse?**
   a) a palace
   b) a shop selling hot pies
   c) a house built for poor people to live in
   d) a theater

6. **Which vegetable did explorers bring back from North America?**
   a) potato
   b) cabbage
   c) carrot
   d) turnip

7. **Which Tudor explorer stole gold from Spanish ships?**
   a) Sir Leonard Falcon
   b) Sir Anthony Warble
   c) Sir Walter Raleigh
   d) Sir Francis Drake

8. **At which age could Tudor girls get married?**
   a) 12
   b) 14
   c) 16
   d) 21

9 **What did ordinary Tudors eat at every meal?**

a) rice
b) cakes
c) bread
d) potatoes

10 **Which Tudor theater was rebuilt in London and reopened in 1997?**

a) the Rose
b) the Swan
c) the Shakespeare
d) the Globe

ANSWERS 1d, 2b, 3c, 4b, 5c, 6a, 7d, 8a, 9c, 10d

FURTHER INFORMATION

BOOKS

Adams, Simon. *Tudor.* London, England: Dorling Kindersley Publishing, 2021.

Deary, Terry. *Terrifying Tudors.* London, England: Scholastic, 2021.

WEBSITES

Britannica Kids: House of Tudor

https://kids.britannica.com/kids/article/Tudor-House-of/476330

Learn more about the Tudors with more facts and photographs.

National Geographic Kids: 10 Facts About The Tudors!

www.natgeokids.com/uk/discover/history/general-history/tudor-facts/

Check out more facts about the Tudors!

Index